Jump, Pup!

Susan B. Neuman

NATIONAL GEOGRAPHIC

Washington, D.C.

Vocabulary Tree

MY BACKYARD

ANIMALS

PETS

PUP

ACTIVITIES

play jump tug run roll catch wag
smell see walk lie nap

This is my pup. Let's play.

Jump, pup!

Tug!

Run.

Roll.

Catch a ball!

Catch a stick!

Wag your tail.

What do you smell?

What do you see?

Let's take a walk.

Let's see some friends.

Lie in the sun.

Yawn!

Take a nap.

YOUR TURN!

Tell a story about a pup.

Paperback ISBN: 978-1-4263-1508-4
Reinforced library edition ISBN: 978-1-4263-1509-1

Book design by David M. Seager

Photo credits
Cover, Tierfotoagentur/Alamy; 1, Close Encounters of the Furry Kind/Kimball Stock; 2–3, Gary Randall/Kimball Stock; 4, Jean-Michel Labat/ARDEA; 5, Jean-Michel Labat/ARDEA; 6, Renee Morris Animal Collection/Alamy; 7, Jean-Michel Labat/ARDEA; 8, Klein-Hubert/Kimball Stock; 9, Johan De Meester/ARDEA; 10–11, Stefanie Krause-Wieczorek/Imagebroker/Biosphoto; 12–13, Jean-Michel Sotto/Kimball Stock; 14–15, Jean-Michel Labat/ARDEA; 16, John Daniels/ARDEA; 17, Close Encounters of the Furry Kind/Kimball Stock; 18–19, Close Encounters of the Furry Kind/Kimball Stock; 20–21, Ron Kimball/Kimball Stock; 22, Gary Randall/Kimball Stock; 23 (top), John Daniels/ARDEA; 23 (puppy), John Daniels/ARDEA; 23 (ball), Stepan Bormotov/Shutterstock; 23 (bottom), Jean-Michel Labat/ARDEA; 24, Sabine Steuwer/Kimball Stock

National Geographic supports K–12 educators with ELA Common Core Resources.
Visit natgeoed.org/commoncore for more information.

Collection copyright © 2017 National Geographic Partners, LLC
Collection ISBN (paperback): 978-1-4263-2791-9
Collection ISBN (library edition): 978-1-4263-2792-6

Printed in the United States of America
17/WOR/1

Pre-reader

Play, Kitty!

Shira Evans

 NATIONAL GEOGRAPHIC

Washington, D.C.

Vocabulary Tree

ANIMALS

CATS

WHAT THEY DO

play   run   swing   stretch   climb   hide   see
swat   eat   lick   clean   cuddle   yawn   sleep

My kitty likes to play.

Run, kitty!

Swing!

Stretch.

Climb.

Let's hide.

Peek-a-boo!

What do you see, kitty?

Swat a bug.

Play with string.

It's time to eat.

Lick to clean.

Let's cuddle.

Yawn.

It's time to sleep.

YOUR TURN!

Draw a line with your finger to match what the kitty does. Then say how you do these things.

CLIMB

SWING

HIDE

RUN

The publisher gratefully acknowledges the expert literacy review of this book by Susan B. Neuman, Ph.D., professor of early childhood and literacy education, New York University.

Trade paperback ISBN: 978-1-4263-2409-3
Reinforced library edition ISBN: 978-1-4263-2410-9

Designed by Sanjida Rashid

Photo Credits
Cover, John Daniels/ardea.com; 1 (CTR), imagebro-ker/Alamy; 2-3 (CTR), Alamy; 4 (CTR), Juniors Bildar-chiv/age fotostock; 5 (CTR), Lambert/Getty Images; 6 (CTR), Gary Randall/Kimball Stock; 7 (CTR), Ron Kimball/Kimball Stock; 8 (CTR), Gary Randall/Kimball Stock; 9 (CTR), Gary Randall/Kimball Stock; 10-11 (CTR), Gary Randall/Kimball Stock; 12-13 (CTR), Photo-SD/Shutterstock; 14-15 (CTR), Ron Kimball/Kimball Stock; 16 (CTR), Oxana Oleynichenko/Alamy; 17 (CTR), Sabine Steuwer/Kimball Stock; 18-19 (CTR), Richard Stacks/Kimball Stock; 20-21 (CTR), Juniors Bildarchiv GmbH/Alamy; 22 (CTR), Zoonar GmbH/Alamy; 23 (UP), Juniors Bildarchiv/age fotostock; 23 (UP CTR), Gary Randall/Kimball Stock; 23 (LO CTR), Ron Kimball/Kimball Stock; 23 (LO), Lambert/Getty Images; 24 (UP), John Daniels/Ardea; 24 (UP), Juniors Bildarchiv/age fotostock; 24 (UP CTR), Gary Randall/Kimball Stock; 24 (LO CTR), Ron Kimball/Kimball Stock; 24 (LO), Lambert/Getty Images

ANSWERS

CLIMB

SWING

HIDE

RUN

Pre-reader

Peek, Otter!

Shira Evans

NATIONAL GEOGRAPHIC

Washington, D.C.

Vocabulary Tree

ANIMALS

RIVER OTTERS

WHAT THEY LOOK LIKE

strong tail
webbed feet

WHAT THEY DO

peek
run
jump
eat
swim
flip
teach
call
sleep

Peek, otter!

Jump!

What's in the river?

Fish

and crabs.

Eat!

An otter has a strong tail.

It has webbed feet.

Swim! Flip!

This otter teaches its baby to find food.

This otter calls out to its baby. Where is it?

Here it is!

It's been a busy day.

Sleep, otter!

Otters teach their babies new things. Adults teach kids new things, too. What are these kids learning?

The answers are on the next page.

The publisher gratefully acknowledges the expert literacy review of this book by Susan B. Neuman, Ph.D., professor of early childhood and literacy education, New York University.

Designed by Sanjida Rashid

Library of Congress Cataloging-in-Publication Data

Names: Evans, Shira, author. | National Geographic Society (U.S.)
Title: Peek, otter / by Shira Evans.
Description: Washington, DC : National Geographic Partners, [2016] | Series:
  National geographic readers | Audience: Ages 2-5.
Identifiers: LCCN 2016005542| ISBN 9781426324369 (pbk. : alk. paper) | ISBN
  9781426324376 (library binding : alk. paper)
Subjects: LCSH: Otters--Juvenile literature.
Classification: LCC QL737.C25 E93 2016 | DDC 599.769--dc23
LC record available at https://lccn.loc.gov/2016005542

Photo Credits

Cover, Andy Rouse/Nature Picture Library; 1, F1online digitale Bildagentur GmbH/Alamy; 2-3, Gerard Lacz/Kimball Stock; 4, Andy Rouse/Nature Picture Library; 5, Andy Rouse/Nature Picture Library; 6-7, Elliott Neep/Minden Pictures; 8, Volodymyr Melnyk/Alamy; 9, Visuals Unlimited, Inc./Fabio Pupin/Getty Images; 10-11, Louis-Marie Preau/Getty Images; 12, David Tipling/Minden Pictures; 13, Marc Chamberlain/SeaPics.com; 14-15, Luciano Candisani/Minden Pictures; 16-17, Arco Images GmbH/Alamy; 18, D. Sheldon/F1 Online/Corbis; 19, Chris Reynolds/Alamy; 20-21, F1online digitale Bildagentur GmbH/Alamy; 22, S.Cooper Digital/Shutterstock; 23 (UP), blue jean images/Getty Images; 23 (UP CTR), Ronnie Kaufman/Larry Hirshowitz/Getty Images; 23 (LO CTR), Westend61/Getty Images; 23 (LO), KidStock/Getty Images; 24 (UP), Arco Images GmbH/Alamy

ANSWERS:

1. How to eat
2. How to read
3. How to play ball
4. How to ride a bike

Go, Cub!

Susan B. Neuman

NATIONAL
GEOGRAPHIC

Washington, D.C.

Vocabulary Tree

ANIMALS

FAMILIES

LIONS

cub mother father
brother sister

CUB ACTIVITIES

go climb hunt
chase pounce
roar growl cuddle
sleep

cub

Meet a lion cub and his family.

mother

He has a mother lion.

father

He has a father lion.

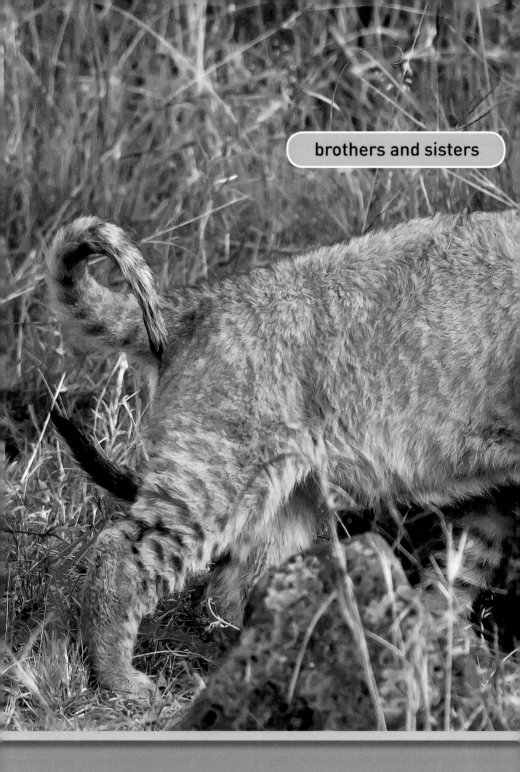

brothers and sisters

He has brothers and sisters.

Go, cub!

Climb!

Learn to hunt.

Chase!

Pounce!

A lion can roar.

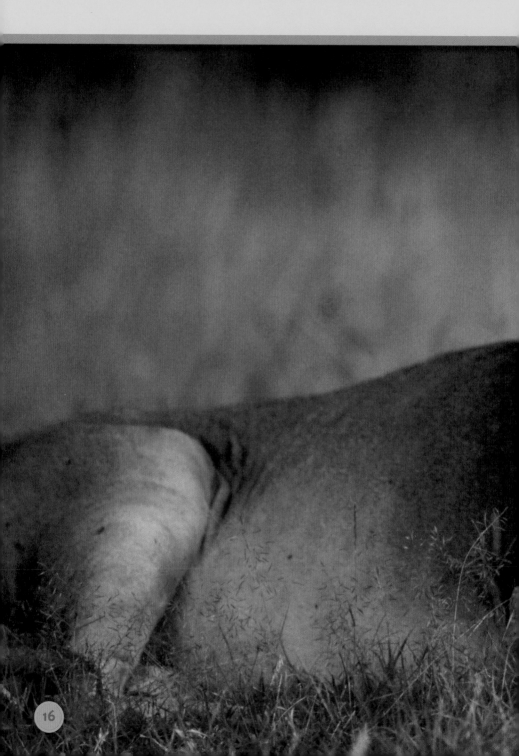

A lion can growl.

But a cub likes to cuddle

and sleep.

Let's go, cub!

What does the cub like to do?

Tell what is happening in this photo.

The answer is on the next page.

Paperback ISBN: 978-1-4263-1512-1
Reinforced library edition ISBN: 978-1-4263-1513-8

Book design by David M. Seager

Photo credits

Cover, Suzi Eszterhas/Minden Pictures; 1, ZSSD/Minden Pictures; 2-3, Frans Lanting/Mint Images/Getty Images; 4-5, Frans Lanting/National Geographic Creative; 6-7, Villiers Steyn/Shutterstock; 8-9, Manoj Shah/The Image Bank/Getty Images; 10, Mitsuaki Iwago/Minden Pictures; 11, Beverly Joubert/National Geographic Creative; 12-13, Suzi Eszterhas/Minden Pictures; 14, MJStone/Shutterstock; 15, Suzi Eszterhas/Minden Pictures; 16-17, Shin Yoshino/Minden Pictures; 18-19, John Carnemolla/Shutterstock; 20-21, Dave Pusey/Shutterstock; 22, Yva Momatiuk & John Eastcott/Minden Pictures; 23, Beverly Joubert/National Geographic Creative; 24, Julian W/Shutterstock

National Geographic supports K–12 educators with ELA Common Core Resources.
Visit natgeoed.org/commoncore for more information.

Answer:
The lion cub is pouncing as it plays. It is learning to be a hunter when it grows up.